My tower

Story by Beverley Randell
Illustrations by Susy Boyer Rigby

My tower is going up.

My tower is going up
and up.

3

No! No!

Down comes my tower.

Here is my big red block.

Here is my big blue block.

My tower is going up.

9

My tower is going

up and up and up!

My little red block

goes here.

My little blue block

goes here.

Look at my big tower!